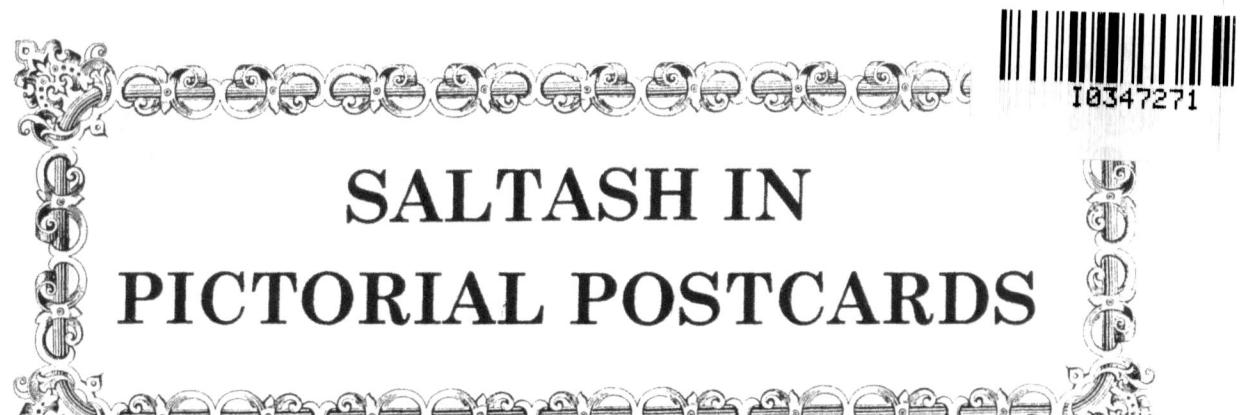

SALTASH IN PICTORIAL POSTCARDS

Tony J. Lucas

Brunels' Rail Bridge over the Tamar
This is Saltash's most well known feature which was erected to the plans of Isambard Kingdom Brunel, engineer to the Great Western Railway, and opened in 1859. This card, dated 1910, also shows the ferry, small sailing boats and a steam train passing under the first arch of the bridge on the Devon side.

This version of the book is virtually as originally published, presenting the work of Tony J Lucas. There are now additional pages at the back providing information about the publisher, Arthur L Clamp.

The republishing project is being managed by Arthur's grandson, Steven Gibson. We aim to find all the research that he was involved in publishing, preserving it for the next generation as part of 'The Clamp Collection'.

INTRODUCTION

There have been thousands of postcards produced almost for all areas of the country since the days of the heavy glass plate camera which was supported on a wooden tripod. The plates were developed and then printed on to photographic paper and etched onto metal printing plates, a process introduced in the 1890s, which opened up a new market for local illustrations. Now over ninety years later an enthusiastic number of people are collecting these cards often forming a collection of a certain topic or the area in which they live such as those printed in this booklet.

The cards, once so common, are now quite rare with prices increasing each year according to the condition, age, and rarity of them. There are many postcard fairs held throughout the country and people go to them looking through large batches in the hope of adding to their own collection. Some were printed locally, such as by Dingles of Saltash, but the majority were produced by large companies sending photographers throughout the country to photograph scenes, towns, people and events. One such company is Friths whose cards have now been reproduced in a large format.

I have lived in Saltash all my life and started collecting postcards some years ago not then realising how many hours this pursuit would occupy and increase my interest in Saltash and also bring me into contact with other collectors in other parts of the country.

I now share part of my collection with you through this booklet and I hope you will find them as interesting as I have in getting hold of rare cards and identifying details of local scenes many of which are now gone forever yet linger in the minds of senior local people.

Acknowledgements

I could not have started this collection without the support of my wife Rose who has spent many hours visiting postcard fairs and flea markets looking out for Saltash cards. She showed great patience and acumen when buying a card especially if it was a rare one. I would also like to take this opportunity to record my many thanks to the following people for their donation of cards and general support in my endeavours at building up a comprehensive collection depicting many aspects of Saltash and its people. Mr. A. C. Powell-Thomas, Mr. G. H. Webber, Mr. D. Whitelock and the late Frank Coombe and William John Peters. Special thanks are also recorded for the work of Heather Tucker who gathered much of the information together and to Arthur L. Clamp who advised me on the best way of getting part of my collection into print.

Tony J. Lucas,
28 Frobisher Drive,
Saltash, Cornwall PL12 4PN

Saltash Crest

Yes, even the town's crest appeared on a postcard many years ago as seen here. I specially cherish this in my collection of local cards. The crest has also appeared on many ceramics, small pots, etc., and was presumably awarded to the town when it gained its borough status.

Saltash Ferry
This Paine card franked in 1905 shows part of the waterside activity with a carrier waiting to board presumably to take goods to Plymouth. The ferry service started in December, 1891.

Dingle Ferry Card
This is franked the 14th July, 1910, and is on the Devon side. The four oil lamps on the ferry are clearly seen; little traffic then with carriers mainly using it for passage across the Tamar to Plymouth.

Driving on the Ferry
The Dodge lorry (JCV 764) was owned by Geo. H. Webber, Ltd., a local building contractor who started on 2nd April, 1935. He recently retired. The last public run of the ferry was on 23rd October, 1961.

Albert Road
This card is dated 1907 showing the view down Albert Road. Cory's butchers shop stands at the bottom of Tamar Street known to outsiders as Pickle Cockle Alley.

Tamar Street
Mr. Kingdom and Ida Downes stand in the doorway of Cory's poultry and meat shop. Opposite the *Tamar Inn* you can just see R. Cook and Co. baker and confectioner's shop with the sun blind.

Embarking for Plymouth
Going aboard the paddle steamer overlooked by the high rail bridge and backed by the industrial training ship *Mount Edgcumbe* which took in over 3,000 boys during its years at the mooring.

Tamar Street
This is a C. A. Pratt card dated 25th June, 1907, looking east towards the *Passage House Inn* showing also A. Pope's grocery and fruitier shop facing a coloured pole on the left side of the street.

Tamar Street
This view is looking east towards Cory's butchers shop. On the left is Annie Pope's cockle shop with tea rooms on the opposite side of the street. The card is franked 1924

Pickle Cockle Alley
The archway with the sign *Passage House Inn* on it was pulled down in 1961 for the redevelopment of Waterside so bringing to an end this once well known narrow thoroughfare in the town. The card is franked 1924.

Saltash Station
This view is westward towards the goods yard with loco no. 4929 going to Swansea at 10.48 a.m. on 24th September, 1957.

Pratt Postcard
The Saltash post mark is clearly seen on this card conveying the message that Miss Scantlebury of Bristol is coming down to Saltash for a few days. No doubt she travelled by train.

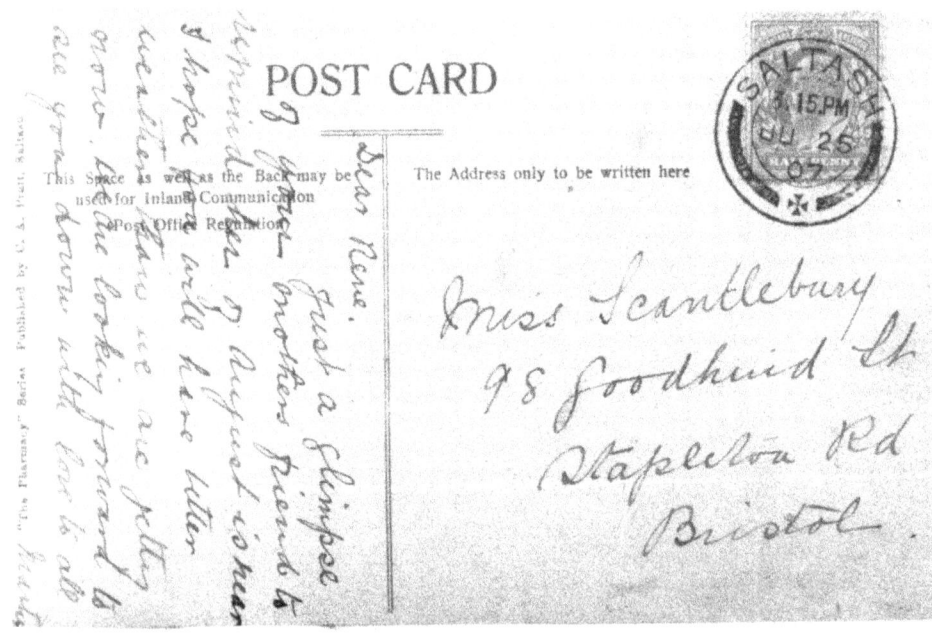

Last Steam Train
It is spring 1961 and one of the last steam trains, no. 5069, crosses Brunel's bridge. Note the construction of the road bridge in the background.

Dingle Card of 1913
This is a very good view of the station showing part of the platform with luggage (two bags are marked *Leeds*) awaiting the next train. Note the *J. F. Prowse* advertisement on the down platform.

Steam Motor Train
This card is franked 1904 showing an early steam motor train operating from Plymouth calling at Saltash and other stations. No unemployment then as many staff were required to maintain this service as grouped here.

Station Footbridge
This was one of my first postcards showing a horse and cart taking away goods from the station. The bridge just north of it was later demolished and re-built nearer the signal box.

7

Mary Newman's Cottage
Situated in Culver Road, this is thought to be the oldest building in Saltash. She lived here before becoming Francis Drake's first wife in 1569 in St. Budeaux church.

Convent of the Good Shepherd
The card is dated 1945 showing the convent buildings on the left and the Roman Catholic church in the middle distance.
The convent was later used as a home for the elderly named St. Anne's Home.

Restoration of the Cottage
An early card showing the cottage before its restoration by the Tamar Protection Society which took place in the 1980s. It is now open to the public on certain days.

St. Nicholas and Faith Church
This Dingle card dated 1917 shows the town's main church whose foundations go back to about the 1200s. Up until 1924 it belonged to the Mayor and Corporation of Saltash who had possession of its key.

Church and Square
The tower lost its battlements in 1930 as part of a restoration scheme and the clock had also changed its face. The Square has been the scene of many public events overlooked by the nearby Guildhall.

Church Interior
Gas jet lighting is seen here in this view during the early years of this century. Many people and events that make up part of the town's heritage are recorded in murals and plaques which make fascinating reading inside the church.

Fore Street

Three views of this central thoroughfare shows the very steep hill running down to the old ferry with the Wesley Mission Hall on the right which later became the Dwelly Hall. The lower length of the hill is backed by the granite arches of the rail viaduct running into the station. It is in the 1920s; no traffic at all, just a quiet Sunday afternoon atmosphere about the place. The lower view dates from the 1930s with children looking at the photographer standing quite safely in the middle of the road with the Masonic Hall on the left.

Upper Fore Street
This is one of the oldest cards in my collection showing the corner of North Road leading off from Fore Street. It was known as *Symons Corner* through Herbert Symon's grocery shop standing there.

Fore Street
This view shows the *Railway Hotel* on the left and Janes shop with meat hanging outside of it. There was even traffic congestion then with many carrier carts delivering goods to the various shops.

Fore Street
This card is post dated 1916 and on the left is seen a delivery boy with a Paines hand cart. Dingle's stationery shop is on the right while further up the same side is the entrance to the *Mansion* later known as the Working Men's Club.

Penn Symons Memorial

These three postcards depict the monument in Victoria Gardens to Major General Sir William Penn Symons, who was the first British general to be killed in the Boer War in South Africa. The plate records "This monument was erected by his countrymen at home and abroad to the memory of Major General Sir William Penn Symons, K.C.B., of Hatt, who fell while commanding the British troops at Talana Hill, Natal, on the 20th October, 1899."

Defiance Halt, 1905-30
The date of this card is the 14th July, 1917, a year when hundreds of naval recruits would alight from trains at this specially built halt for their training on the old wooden hulk. This is a Dingle card.

H.M.S. Defiance
This card records low tide showing the torpedo school ship training vessel which was first moved to Wearde Quay in 1884 where there was a custom post and gate.

H.M.S. Defiance
This Dingle card gives a closer view of the training vessel from where in 1903 the young sailors formed a bucket train from the river when Wearde House was on fire. Part of the house was saved due to their prompt action.

Military Church Parade, October 1914
Headed by a band hundreds of recruits march from church parade possibly across Cross Park. War was declared against Austria on 12th August, 1914, so these local men are likely to be part of the first intake into that gruesome conflict. How many returned from the fighting in the trenches one can only hazard a guess.

St. Stephen's Vicarage Lawn Party
This gathering of bonneted ladies and girls with boys in best clothes and wearing polished boots probably dates just after the start of the First World War. Few men are shown, the garden is bedecked with flags but the occasion has gone unrecorded.

St. Stephens
This card is dated 1905 when St. Stephens was the centre of a very large parish and the Borough of Saltash was just a fraction of its size. The *Cecil Arms* public house on the right looks over the large open central area useful for many public events.

St. Stephen's Church
Largely unaltered since the 1550s this stone building replaced an earlier of which records go back to the 1200s. There are many memorials to local people along the walls which make interesting reading.

Interior of St. Stephen's
Granite columns, a high pulpit, gas lighting, the nave and pews facing the altar once separated by a wooden screen, typify the interior of many parish churches around the turn of this century.

Forder Post Office
This wooden building, used as the hamlet's post office, was in the grounds of Forder Villa and from about 1915 to 1925 was also used as tea rooms and stores when it was moved to the grounds of Apple Tree Cottage

Forder, St. Stephens
This card is franked 1905 and shows Forder as it must have looked for hundreds of years. The house on the right was the post office seen here with a postman standing in front of it

Apple Tree Cott
Day trippers often came to Forder by paddle steamer from Plymouth to visit this popular tea garden between 1891 and 1938. It was reckoned to be the best garden around Saltash. Here are seen a family of four standing in front of the cottage.

The Ploughboy Inn Darts Club

This enlarged card shows the team at Burraton who were runners up in *The Peoples Darts 1950* competition. Shown here left to right back row is unknown, Bill Gray, Ted Gray, unknown, Peter Gray, unknown, unknown, Cliff Veale, lady unknown, unknown, Tug Wilson. Front row: All unknown except Charlie Lock. If anyone can help in naming these people I would be very pleased.

St. Stephen's Football Team 1938-39

This other enlarged postcard shows the pre-war team made up of Bill Blewitt, Bob Hallet, Ern Alford, Norman Barriball, Albert Nicholson, Donald Clark, Charlie Jonas and Ted Gifford in the back row then Reg Hodge, Fred Crosley, Bill Bryant, George Cook, Ern Bryant, in the middle row, and lastly Horace (Bill) Hodge, Reg Allen, Collie Hodge, Les Hodge, Victor Manning and Fred Pickard.

Slade Gardens. Whit Monday 1915.

Slade Tea Gardens

Fortunately the top enlarged postcard has been dated for Whit Monday, 1915, which clearly shows the popularity of the gardens and swings on a public holiday. It was certainly the place to take the children and spend a few hours with them here which could be reached on foot from most local homes. The gardens were situated between North Road and old Ferry Road which gave good views towards Dartmoor over the river upon which is moored an old ship's hulk. The lower enlarged card gives a closer view of the swing boats.

SWING BOATS, SLADE TEA GARDENS SALTASH.

Rustic Tea Gardens

These very rare cards, one franked 1909, show a once popular setting for a day's outing for local people especially on Bank holidays. The use of entwined branches to form a spider's web shape made these gardens distinctive in the area. The proprietor was a Mr. F. Newbury.

Message on Card
Dear Mother,
I am over to Saltash for the afternoon in what they call the rustic tea gardens. It is a lovely little place, this is one of the shady corners.
From Sam.
(Sent to Mrs. Stabb, Brixham.)

County School 1927
Built in that year to accommodate increasing numbers of local pupils it was later known as the Saltash Grammar School; it is now St. Stephen's Primary School. The card is dated 1946.

North Road
It is 1950, the van belongs to Tom Stanlake, a local farmer, which is carrying a milk churn. His brother Chris also had a milk round. Les Davey's cycle shop and Seccombe's bakery were demolished to make way for the new bridge in 1961. The school stood where the road now runs into the tunnel.

Just One Car
It is the 1950s again and the card shows Lower Lollabury now known as New Road, Saltash then with very little traffic. The bungalows were built in the 1930s.

CALLINGTON CIRCUIT "LOCAL PREACHERS" SERIES 1906
Mr. Canning Vosper,
SALTASH.

CALLINGTON CIRCUIT "LOCAL PREACHERS" SERIES, 1906.
Mr. Harold A. Hosking,
LANDRAKE.

Local Personalities

Postcards sometimes depict local people in addition to the usual scenes. Here three preachers are shown serving the congregations in Methodist chapels in and around Saltash. These are Mr. W. B. H. Stephens, Saltash, Mr. Canning Vosper, Saltash, and Mr. Harold A. Hosking of Landrake. The chapels are grouped into circuits and preachers had to make their own way (without cars) to fulfil their appointments as listed in a quarterly plan of services throughout the circuit.

Often a family in a village chapel would invite the preacher for Sunday lunch when he was planned to take the normal two Sunday services and then make his own way home after the evening service.

Alexandra Pleasure Steamer
This was one of three vessels owned by the Saltash, Three Towns and District Steamboat Company which ran from 1892 to 1910. This steamer was built in 1888 and was broken up in 1927-28

A Glimpse of the Gas Holder
This is just in the picture and stood alongside Waterside from where the town obtained its gas. It is long gone, the Saltash Sailing club premises now stand close to its site. A paddle steamer is moored offshore probably out of service for the moment.

At Rest and Play
Although this card is franked 1917 it is probably much older. Local boats are beached or moored at Waterside, two boatmen are resting and two children are playing among them. A ferry steamer waits for passengers alongside the old pontoon.

Fore Street in the late 1940s

Looking down Saltash's main street a few years after the end of the Second World War showing the Regal cinema on the left facing Cory's butchers shop and Fenton's off licence. The lower postcard view is looking up Fore Street with Underhill's chemist shop, still in business, opposite Rounsell Bros. shop. All the premises on the right were demolished for road widening and the re-development of the shopping centre as seen today.

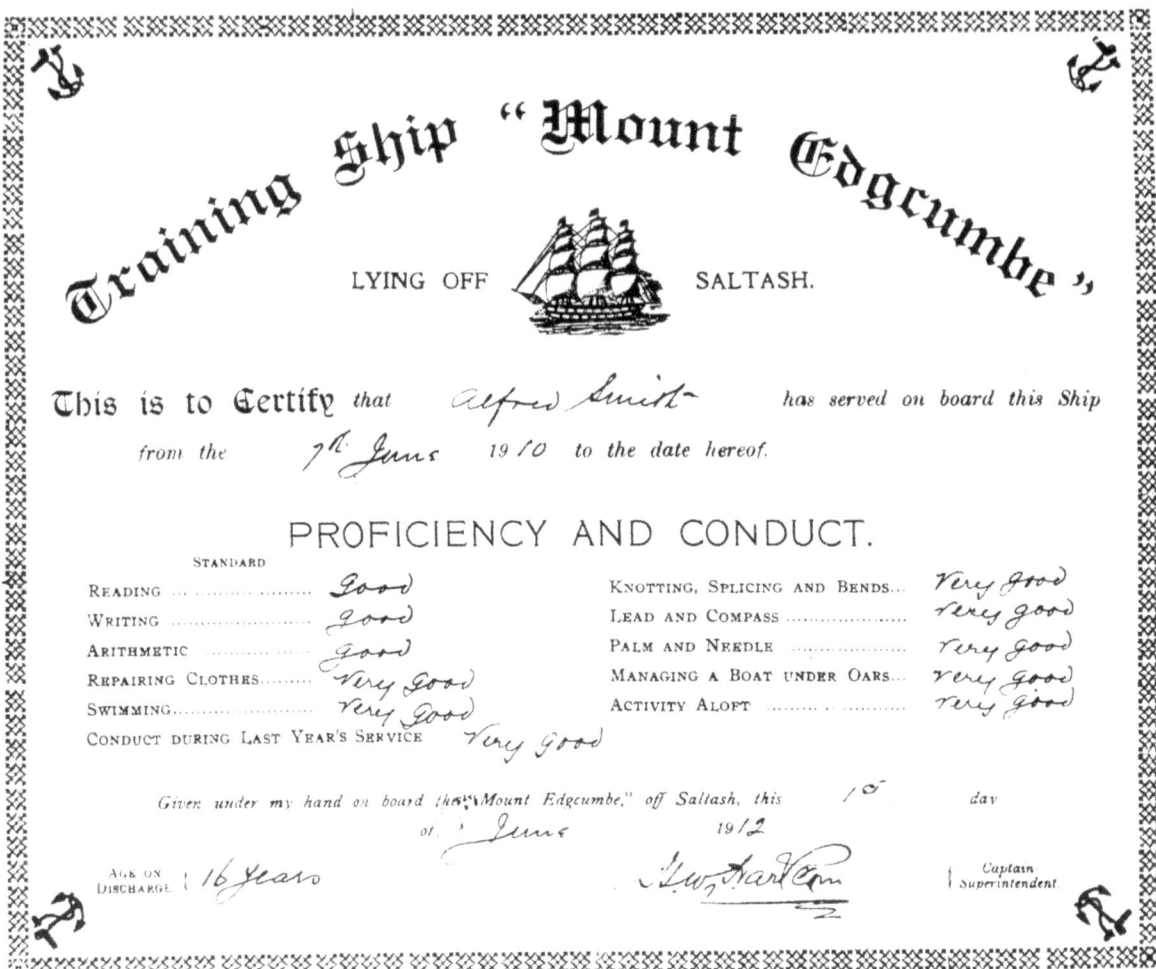

Serving the young people of Saltash

These are not postcards but complete this book by recording two local well known enterprises in the service of young people. A leaving certificate of the training ship *Mount Edgcumbe*, dated 1912, for Alfred Swift could have been for one of the local boys. The foundation stone laying date is recorded for the still popular boys' club which was later officially opened by Frankie Vaughan. Girls now make about half of its membership.

 SALTASH BOYS' CLUB

Foundation Stone Laying Ceremony

by

H.M. LORD LIEUTENANT OF CORNWALL

Colonel Sir JOHN CAREW POLE, Bart., D.S O., T.D., J.P., C.A.

SATURDAY, 30th MAY, 1964 at 3 p.m.

Arthur L. Clamp – the man behind the books

Arthur Leslie Clamp was a man of boundless energy with a passion for helping others, particularly through his love of history. A printer by trade, he started his career in a printing company before moving his family from Exeter to Plymouth to teach at the Plymouth College of Art and Design, where he eventually became the Head of the Printing Department.

Arthur with his five children.

A Devoted Family Man

Despite his love of teaching, Arthur prioritised his family, always making it home by 5:30pm for tea. He and his wife, Rosemary, raised five children: Susan, Angela, Elizabeth, David, and Steven. Arthur would often combine his love of family and history by taking his children on Sunday walks, encouraging them to appreciate historical monuments by taking photos or making crayon rubbings of gravestones for his books. The family home at 203 Elburton Road was a hub of activity, with a large garden, featuring a two-storey fort and a makeshift swimming pool.

A Lifelong Learner and Adventurer

Arthur's thirst for knowledge extended beyond history to a deep curiosity about the world. He was passionate about exploring different cultures, traditions, and cuisines, often taking advantage of his long summer holidays as a teacher to travel to places like India, Russia, South America, the middle east and the USA, sometimes bringing one of his children along. This adventurous spirit even influenced his home life, as seen by the short-lived family tradition of steam-cooking vegetables after a trip to Iceland.

History is a prominent feature of family days out

Community and Philanthropic Spirit

His commitment to serving others was evident in his long-standing involvement with the Elburton Methodist Church. He was the Sunday School Superintendent for over 15 years and served as the editor of the wider church's monthly newsletter, "The Link," for a similar duration. After Rosemary's very sad passing, Arthur later remarried and, following a chance encounter with a professor from India, established a connection with a missionary school in Chennai. Together with his new wife, Christine, he co-founded a "Sponsor a Child's Education" program that continues to this day.

Pictured left – The cover of 'The Link' complete with hand drawn sketches of each church by Angela
Below right – Arthur Clamp promoting his latest book
Below left – Arthur at home with his first wife, Rosemary
Below centre – Arthur on holiday with his second wife, Christine

A Legacy of Learning and Positivity

Arthur's greatest passion was history, which he brought to life through tireless research, documentation, and the many books he authored. He was driven by a need to "never be stuck in a rut," constantly seeking new experiences, meeting new people, and expanding his knowledge. With a positive attitude and a great sense of humour, he was always ready to help others, leaving a lasting impact on his family and community. His children, Susan, Angela, Elizabeth, David, and Steven, remember him with love and gratitude.

David Clamp, 2025

A Legacy of Local History

Below is the story of how Arthur L Clamp began writing books, in his own words, drafted shortly before he passed away in 2001. I have only made minor alterations to this text, correcting grammatical errors that he did not survive to correct himself. When I first discovered this text, I was shocked to see my name mentioned. It seems that, unbeknownst to me, I shared my first PC with him. I suspect he used it during the day when I was at school, although I do have one memory of sitting with him and showing him how it worked. It has been a pleasure to pick up where he left off and see his books republished and redistributed, and to know that I was part of the story, even back then. It was also fascinating to discover that his pricing structure matches the way I have tried to price the books, with a third going to local sellers and the rest covering printing costs with a little left over for my expenses.

I am his eldest grandson, and it is a privilege to curate his legacy, which we are calling 'The Clamp Collection'. The very last line of the text originally reads "The following pages list all the titles." Sadly, that page is missing and we have no record of all the books he published and knowing that some of those were researched by other authors makes the process of finding them even harder. I look forward to one day completing the collection and seeing them all available again. And maybe, one day, I'll even start writing my own to add to the series. For now, here is his story in his own words.

Steven Gibson, 2025

Writing and Publishing Booklets on Local Topics and Areas

I started this interest in either 1968 or 1969 when living in Woodford. I had by these dates established the Department of Printing and I think I must have been looking for something different to do. The first titles were of A5 size proofed from type set at Clarke, Doble and Brendon, Ltd., Plymouth printers, and then made up into pages and printed at Sawtell and Neilson, Ltd., Totnes.

Then began a slow process of getting them out to shops, etc. which proved to be more time consuming and difficult than actually researching, writing and getting the books into print. However, I persisted and opened a business account with Barclays Bank on the Broadway. I was advised to give it a title so I called it "Westway Publications". There came along another problem, one of storage of paper and finished books which was solved when the family moved to Elburton in 1970.

I changed the printer to Penwell, Ltd., Callington, Cornwall, as he was then just setting up himself and his prices seemed very reasonable. I did not get any of the printers to make up the complete books. I hand folded the flat printed sheets, stitched the books on a small manual table stitcher and trimmed them in a small hand turned guillotine which I bought from someone in Penzance for £40. It was brought up in a van.

The trouble and time going to and fro to Callington was too much so I transferred the printing to PDS Printers, Prince Rock, Plymouth, and I have been with them ever since. Now they are at Plympton which is easy to reach and they fold the flat sheets which was turning out to be a long chore which only saved a small part of the printing costs.

All my first titles were written by myself. I took the photographs and developed them in the loft of the house, the type was set by now on a computer situated in the house at Elburton from which I had collected photographic lengths of text to cut up and law down as pages.

At some point I decided that I would do my own film processing of lith film so I bought a large second hand process camera from Kingsbridge and learnt through trial and error to make line negatives of the text and halftone negatives of the illustrations which proved more difficult than I anticipated. The main problem was trying to keep the developer in the large dish at the correct temperature as any change would affect the developing time. I replaced this old camera with a brand new one bought from Croydon, Surrey, costing £900. This has turned out to be a great asset cutting out an expensive part of the printer's costs and one crucial aspect of the work which I could control.

By the middle 1970s there were many outlets I had contacted in Plymouth, up to Dartmoor, Exeter, around to Torbay, Totnes, Dartmouth and the South Hams. The market for local books was much greater than I had first thought and through getting to know many local people undertaking research themselves had the chance to help and make up books for other people who had in most instances, got together a collection of photographs with some text in a rather muddled way. Through my experience in print I was able to shape up their work and get it into print and in every case I had to pay the printer and let the person have the royalties. In the majority of titles produced in this manner this was another way of producing titles and it did give some profit to my work. However, I must say that in a few cases I lost out by either the other person getting the numbers wrong, not returning any monies from stock I delivered or they thought that more of their books should have been sold.

The print run was usually 1,000 copies and from time to time I have had reprints of 250 copies. It took about ten years to clear the first print run so I always had large stocks in the garage, workshop, etc. The numbers sold during the early years was about 7,000 copies a year increasing to around 9,000 copies and for the whole of the enterprise about 500,000 have been sold. The booklets have become part of the local scene and many people collect them, shops regularly order copies and I go around certain areas month by month restocking or replacing titles as necessary.

During the past year or so I have started setting the text on a Packard Bell PC, something which I should have done some years back. I share it with Steven Gibson, my grandson. There appears to be no end to the market for local books, but I could not earn a regular income because of the long time it takes to sell stock.

However, now exceeding 100 titles made up mainly of A4 twenty-four page booklets, some folded guides, with selling prices set with a third going to the shop which is the trade custom, the original idea has been quite successful and could go on for ever.

Apart from monetary benefits, however spasmodically these might be, I have learnt a lot myself, met many interesting people and have become part of the local scene with requests to give talks and to advise people about getting into print.

Arthur L Clamp, 2001

This newspaper article, published by the Evening Herald on 17th August 2001, forms a good record of his life. Just as he encourages us to learn more about local history, we encourage you to learn a little about him. For that reason, we have included these pages at the back of all the most recently republished books, in honour of his memory and recognition of his contribution to the community.

www.ingramcontent.com/pod-product-compliance
Lightning Source LLC
Chambersburg PA
CBHW061408070526
44584CB00031B/4190